T0194423

A Chariot To God
Through The Mercy of Jesus

Poems by
Jessie Marquis

WESTBOW
P R E S S®
A DIVISION OF THOMAS NELSON
& ZONDERVAN

WestBow Press books may be ordered through booksellers or by contacting:

WestBow Press
A Division of Thomas Nelson & Zondervan
1663 Liberty Drive
Bloomington, IN 47403
www.westbowpress.com
1 (866) 928-1240

ISBN: 978-1-9736-0746-5 (sc)
ISBN: 978-1-9736-0745-8 (e)

Library of Congress Control Number: 2017917359

Print information available on the last page.

WestBow Press rev. date: 10/01/2019

God speaks creation into existence operating between time and space

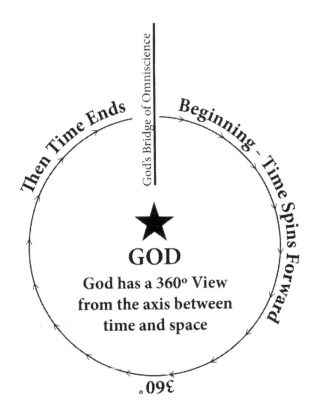

GOD

God has a 360° View
from the axis between
time and space

God's Bridge of Omniscience

Then Time Ends

Beginning - Time Spins Forward

360°

-- HE IS THE GREAT I AM --
The Truth, The Light, and The Way,
By Whom All Things Were Created.

A CHARIOT TO GOD
– His Complete Plan –

A gift from God
A vision of glory
A descendant of truth
of a righteous story

From an ancient time of Adam and Eve
to future events which mankind believe

God blessed us all with living soul,
And gifted us hope and made us whole.

As the guiding star of the heavens above,
Pointed the world the Savior's love.

He washed our souls from our sins,
Started our lives as new hope begins.

To walk with our Savior hand in hand
as trumpeters of truth to unite the land.

We rescue the sheep in the name of His love
that binds the Church to heaven above.

From the fountain of youth to a future day,
the events of time rapidly pendulum away.

For the key to the universe just words apart,
From the sword of God to a believer's heart,
    Is carried on in the name of the dove,
    that weds the church our Savior's love.

To the children of the son of all the lands,
A Chariot to God through guiding hands.

BEGINNING

5.

God's fallen fruit cast down upon the tree of knowledge
–– the knowledge of good and evil ––
as sin is represented as the top of the jar.
To seal the jar is represented as spiritual
separation, then death.

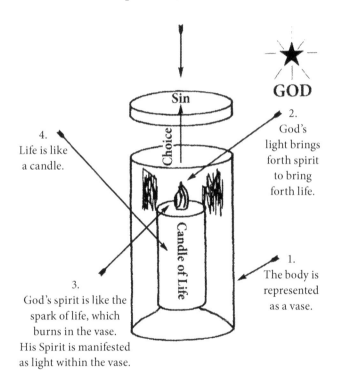

GOD

Sin

Choice

Candle of Life

4.
Life is like
a candle.

2.
God's
light brings
forth spirit
to bring
forth life.

1.
The body is
represented
as a vase.

3.
God's spirit is like the
spark of life, which
burns in the vase.
His Spirit is manifested
as light within the vase.

O'EVIL LIAR TEMPTED EVE'S DESIRE

O'Evil Liar, tempted Eve's desire,

To bring forth war within.

From the depth of sin

did war begin

as his seed multiplied within.

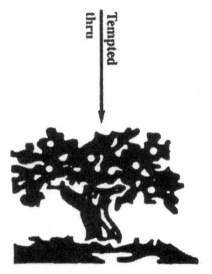

Tempted
thru

THE TREE OF KNOWLEDGE
AND DISOBEDIENCE

Satan's way of trying to put his throne above God's

Throne Room - God's Light

Seven Characteristics in Man as Seen on Page 5, No. 2

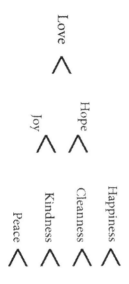

Love
∧

Joy   Hope
∧   ∧

Peace   Kindness   Cleanness   Happiness
∧   ∧   ∧   ∧

Through the tree of knowledge came death, as seen on page 5, No. 5

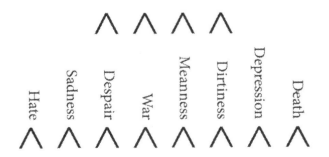

∧   ∧   ∧   ∧

Hate   Sadness   Despair   War   Meanness   Dirtiness   Depression   Death
∧   ∧   ∧   ∧   ∧   ∧   ∧   ∧

Satan's Harness
and many other sins that separate God from us ...
But we are reunited through
the Atonement of Jesus

I turn these eyes asunder
Through love and peace I strive
The star's eyes often wonder
Upon the midnight skies.

NEW Testament

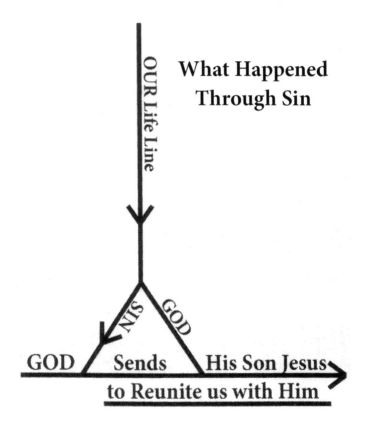

What Happened
Through Sin

OUR Life Line

NTS   GOD

GOD   Sends   His Son Jesus
to Reunite us with Him

John 3:16
For God so loved the world, that he
gave his only begotten Son,
that whosoever believeth in him should not perish,
but have everlasting life.

On Christmas Night Pointed the Guiding Light
The Guiding Star giveth direction
through Most Holy Light has conceived
Through God's Light his projection
Brought forth His Son on Christmas Eve.
As God's son, His reflection,
Who died on the cross for those who believe.
Through His blood comes resurrection
And eternal life we shall receive.

GOD The Son
God and Jesus are One and The Same
-- without sin --

Jesus relights the wicks of life,
and casts sin into Hell,
Then Rises Indeed!

The Way, The Truth, and The Life

INNER MAN, MIRROR MAN

Before I lay down to rest
To the Son of God, I do confess
For the road of life is dark with sin.
But the guiding light doth shine within.

Convicted, thought in the depth of sin.
Repentance through the Son of Man,
To bring forth light to see within,
To interface as a mirror man.

For a star is born in the void of night,
As manifested thought transforms to light.
A soldier of love does travel afar,
To become one with the stars.

He is The Light within us. We are light through Him.

REBORN

I have the key to Heaven
Jesus has shown me the way.
Before I eat my manna,
I read it every day.

To live my life with Jesus
He leads me not astray,
To feel such inner peace,
When I take my time to pray.

To live my life so happily,
To live my life for sure.
To read my Bible daily,
Makes my spirit become mature.

So when people come and ask me,
Why I'm here today?
I simply smile and say to them,
To take my time and pray.

THE GIFT AMONG ALL GIFTS
The gift among all gifts came from Heaven above.
It was written among the stars and
shown by our Savior's love.
So crown him King of kings, most
high from up above,
God's gift he gives to thee --
salvation with eternal love.
So find more joy in giving
this gift you will receive
If you remember while you're living
God's gift on Christmas Eve.

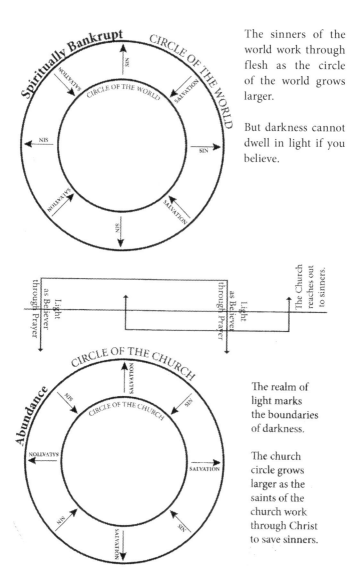

The sinners of the world work through flesh as the circle of the world grows larger.

But darkness cannot dwell in light if you believe.

The realm of light marks the boundaries of darkness.

The church circle grows larger as the saints of the church work through Christ to save sinners.

Road of Life

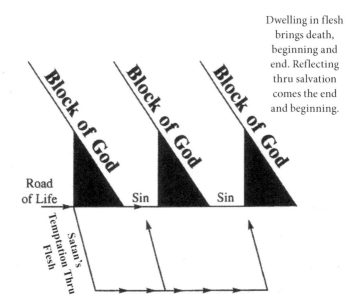

Dwelling in flesh brings death, beginning and end. Reflecting thru salvation comes the end and beginning.

Walker by Night, Seeker of Day

One who is one with God, Is won through Christ.
But if he walks in worldly ways,
forsaking the light of day,
Then he walks by night and not by day,
Stumbling and seeking guidance in
the light of God once again.

Revival, Through Prayer!

NEW CREATIONS

LET GOD BE YOUR LINEBACKER
The greatest victory came from the stars above,
He is Heaven's candle light, the reflection of God's love.
So let God be your linebacker,
through the winds of change.
As He brought forth light to all of us,
through His beloved Son's name.
For you see the finer things in life
are not of the human race.
So ride the wings of the Dove, through
his beloved Son to grace.

–– THREE in One, One and the same ––

FOR GOD SENT HIS SON JESUS CHRIST

I'm living the way which I have foreseen
as it approaches Easter Day.
As He hung on the cross for all of us
and died and passed away.
A walk through life as shown by Him
as the trail of time goes by,
To live our life as Christians live
many years did pass us by.
For this traveling Man down the road
of life did light the darkened way,
And paid the price with His very
blood as comes our final day.
Now time is near for trumpet day.
Are you ready for it to come?
Or will you be left behind in a trail of tears
to suffer for what you have done?

**If you truly believe and repent in Jesus' name,
then the Holy Spirit is within you.
HE is the way in which you believe!**

Plugged Into The Power Source

Tethered In Believing

THE UNIFICATION

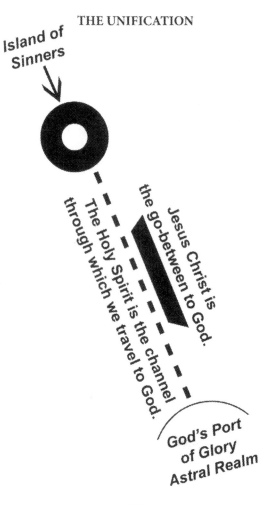

Island of Sinners

Jesus Christ is the go-between to God.

The Holy Spirit is the channel through which we travel to God.

God's Port of Glory Astral Realm

Jesus said, "No man goes to the Father except through me, for I am the gateway."

J

GATEWAY

S

U

S

Revelation the Rapture
Harmony of the Golden Trumpet

So hearken for the trumpet to the wedding He brings,
To bestow upon you this diamond ring.
As bearer of the crown
The King of kings that bonds the church
To no mortal bounds,
From the breath of life to higher ground.
His love shines as a star in the night.
A perfect reflection of God's holy light.

Concept of the Inner Mind Thru Christ

Inward toils the void
Where all the worlds are blind.
Where the darkness surrounds the light
In universal minds.
Seven stars represent the churches
The lights of ALL mankind.
As outward pushes the lights
Through the stream of time,
A reflection upon the sea of life.
Through the way came devotion
When through the fog thus came this night
Upon a stormy ocean.
So we leave our shells to set a sail
Through darkness that clouds our minds.
As through the window a candle light
Through God we love and find.

The seven stars are the churches,
Revolving around the cross.
As He is The light within us
We are light through Him
In the Body of Jesus Christ.

— Roll Call —
The Rapture
of the Church

Harmony in the Guiding Light

I saw the guiding star pass through a window in outer space.
And sitting on a throne, light coming from this place.
In the depth of a cold winter night,
He descended to the human race.
The guiding star represented Jesus, and His trail to grace.
As He wrote in a purple haze,
In the depth of our minds.
To the church it is written,
A promise He left behind.
To soar as an angel among the stars
We leave the flesh behind.
To become a candlelight of inner peace,
Through Jesus Christ we find.
And then the guiding star went nova.
In the depth of the cold winter night,
In the harmony of Gabriel's trumpet,
The church was drawn to the light.

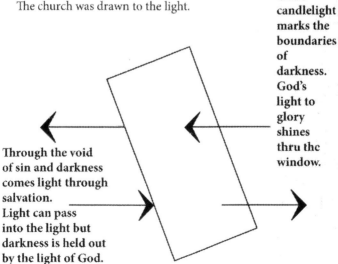

God's candlelight marks the boundaries of darkness. God's light to glory shines thru the window.

Through the void of sin and darkness comes light through salvation. Light can pass into the light but darkness is held out by the light of God.

Tribulation

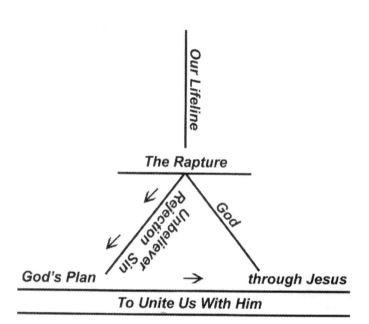

Repentance

In heart an appaloosa,
The world is by our side.
Our worldly ways are many,
Our range both broad and wide.
The world is on our shoulders,
Whose range is both broad and wide.
Our spots are loved by many,
For reasons God's Son did die.
In heart an appaloosa,
The world has left our side.
Our boundaries marked by many,
Through love and peace we strive.
When the world is on our shoulders.
Whose range is both broad and wide.
In heart an appaloosa,
The Lord is by our side.

Hollywood and the Roaming Star

I was born a roaming star,
one with watchful eyes.
To roam the city of neon lights
and watch the stars go by.
The world has no boundaries
for one with watchful eyes.
Because I was born a roaming star,
and the Lord has heard my cry.
Yes, I was born a roaming star,
God's Son has set me free.
Yes, I was born a roaming star,
But God's Light shined on me.
I don't bother with worldly things much,
for God has set me free.
And when all the stars come out at night
Watching is where I'll be.

-- THE LIGHT OF THE WORLD --
Jesus Christ Super Star
Blessed are we, the children of the night.
For the divine star Child and His redeeming light.
Who died on the cross for our sins.
From the beginning of time 'til it ends.
That we may see the eternal glory shining
through this righteous story.
The light that shines by his grace, without
a blemish to the human race.
So we can see without a doubt that trust
in Him is what life is about.
By His Grace we are saved!

-- REVIEWING --
He is Alpha and Omega – The Beginning and End

He is the beginning and the end.
The angels are his lights.
The sea reflects the skies.
The dust becomes the flesh.
His light became the spirit within the man.
Mankind chose to eat of the tree of knowledge.
His fallen fruit, the knowledge of good and evil,
Which determined separation, then salvation.
He is the Truth, the Light, and the Way!
Which is the light, within the Church.
He is seven to become one within the Church,
The Church are his lights, to unite us
through Jesus Christ with the Father.
The Stars reflect his light,
His reflection, Jesus Christ, yielded up the Holy Spirit
to return back to the Father.
Sin is of the Flesh, but Salvation is of God.
Bought and paid for by the blood of Jesus Christ.
His Salvation brings forth light, and light is of God,
God's light brings forth spirit.
Just as He is The light within us,
We are light through Him.
To unite in the Name of the Father,
the Son and the Holy Spirit.
In the house of the Lord, Forever and Ever.
Amen.

JUDGEMENT AND CROWNING

Creation ends its 360° rotation from
the beginning to the end,
then starts its 360° rotation over,
as judgment of sinners,
and crowning of saints from beginning to end.
Through our faithfulness comes our rewards.

OLD HEAVENS

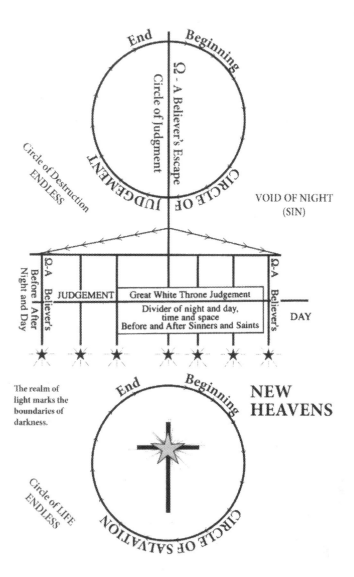

The realm of light marks the boundaries of darkness.

Through GOD Made Flesh As Shown

Sweet Victory Triumph Over Sins

Long reign, long reign, most high God,
Who gave His Son for me.
Who will always reign, Who saveth my soul,
Who died on the cross for me.
Who loveth much, Who giveth much,
Who shed His blood for me.
Long reign, long reign God Most High,
Who giveth His Son for me.
Upward, upward. I will travel upward
so dense are the clouds of night.
The clouds of sin from war within
As to blot out the realm of light.
Who hath the sign within their mind,
Whose blood broke the spell of night.
Who believeth in Him is not condemned.
Through a rainbow the guiding light.
Who believeth in He, He forgiveth thee,
Who divided day from night, Who saved my soul
Who made men whole,
Through He, the realm of light.
Shout "God is Glorious, God is Victorious"
Who reigns the sands of time.
Through magnificent power, doth come the hour.
God's city of the great divine.
Sing praises, quote phrases, as infinite as light within.
For the last and final trumpet call
Has sounded over sin.

God's City of Great Divine breaks down,
God's magnificent light, like a prism
of stones and gems, into aura of colors
of sunshine like a rainbow.

**Salvation By Grace
Not By Works**

Merry Christmas

Many years ago on a cold winter night,
Three wise men were guided by a bright starry light.
They followed the star from far, far away,
To a baby in a manger asleep on the hay.
This baby boy was Jesus and He grew into a man,
To deliver us all from Satan's evil hand.
He came to earth on Christmas Day,
Then died on Easter on a cross far away.
This Baby in a manger saved us from our sins.
Good tidings to all,
And Merry Christmas to man.

Jess Marquis"
Isola, MS
Reborn 1993

And now abideth faith, hope, and love,
but the greatest of all is love in the Family of God.